ETIQUETTE FOR WOMEN

ETIQUETTE FOR WOMEN

A BOOK OF MODERN MANNERS AND CUSTOMS

BY

IRENE DAVISON

CHANCELLOR PRESS

First published in 1928 by C. Arthur Pearson, Ltd

Reprinted 1929, 1933, 1939

This 2002 edition published by Chancellor Press,
an imprint of Bounty Books, a division of
Octopus Publishing Group,
2–4 Heron Quays, London E14 4JP

Reprinted in 2002, 2003, 2004, 2008

ISBN 978 0 753704 14 1

Printed and bound in Germany by GGP Media GmbH, Pößneck

* Please note this is a facsimile edition therefore titles mentioned on the back
of this book may no longer be in print.

CONTENTS

FOREWORD

" BE considerate, and you will be courteous and correct," is a kindly truism, but helpful up to a certain point only. Consideration for others is without question the basis of all etiquette . . . but it is apt to leave us stranded when we want to know the correct way to eat grape-fruit, or how many cards to leave when returning a call.

The woman anxious to solve such everyday problems as these has no need of generalizations : her desire to know those things which make life a pleasanter, more smoothly running affair for everybody is a proof of her innate courtesy. But she does seek help over the details that make up everyday etiquette : what to do in given circumstances, and how, and when. Happily there are certain rules, simple and clearly defined, to guide her : this volume is designed to set out for her the more important of those in common use.

CHAPTER I

INTRODUCTIONS

THREE very simple rules are the basis of all introductions. If you are inclined to get stage fright when you have to introduce people one to another, just learn these rules by heart, and then practise them regularly. Naturally, you can't buttonhole your friends and acquaintances and introduce them haphazard just for your own education: here's a more practical plan.

Every day think of two people at random, characters from a story or the newspaper columns. Introduce them to one another. If you can make the introduction aloud, so much the better. You will learn in this way to apply your rules quickly to all kinds of circumstances ; then, when you wish to make an actual introduction, you won't have to hesitate at the crucial moment to wonder : " Let me see, *whose* name do I mention first ? "

It is worth taking trouble over this point, for

to be able to make introductions easily and gracefully gives self-confidence in many social emergencies.

Like most rules, these have their exceptions, but don't bother yourself with them until you are quite sure of the rules themselves, which cover practically all everyday needs.   They are :

(1) Always introduce the gentleman to the lady, and mention her name first, like this : " Miss Carter, may I introduce Mr. Lester to you ? "

(2) Introduce an unmarried woman to one who is married, and the bachelor to a married man, *but* . . .

(3) When both are married, or both single, introduce the younger to the elder.

Don't make any exception to the first rule, no matter now much more important the man is socially (always and only excepting if he should be a Royal Prince).

To the other two rules, rank does sometimes make a difference.   If one of the two to be introduced be of much higher social standing, the other should be introduced to him or her. And age may modify the second rule, for when the unmarried person is very much the senior it is permissible, and often more gracious, to introduce the younger. It would be better, for example, to introduce a newly-married girl to a distinguished elderly lady who is unmarried.

What to say is a very easy matter : the simple form already suggested is the best to use. But *how* you say it is most important, for you must pronounce the names so clearly that neither of the people introduced will be left wondering what the other's name really is . . . always an embarrassing thing.

When introducing personal friends you may be less formal, but no less punctilious about names. You might say : " Joan, may I introduce Miss Carter to you ; she was my great chum at college." And to the other : " You have often heard me speak of my friend, Mrs. Lely." But you must mention *both surnames* clearly, so that the two will know how to address one another.

If you introduce two friends, say, at a party, and leave them to talk together, do be kind to them and suggest an opening for conversation. If you add, for instance : " Miss Trent thinks of spending her holidays at Tremezzo, where you enjoyed yourself so much," or, " I have been telling Mrs. Tatham about your lovely garden : she is as interested in gardening as you are," you will have started the conversational ball rolling.

If you are out in the street with a friend, and meet another, shall you introduce them ? Well, it isn't necessary, and although there's no fixed rule about it, it is considered better not to make such an introduction. Should the friend you meet stop to speak, your companion would walk on quietly, and let you overtake her. But if you would like the friends to know one another, and think it would please them, too, you will be acting quite correctly in introducing them when you meet : this is often the most natural and graceful thing to do.

There's an " extra " rule about introductions that you must never break. If you are asked for an introduction to someone you know, you must first find out whether that someone is willing to have the introduction made. It is a very grave mistake not to do so . . . and, of course, you would never dream, would you, of asking such permission in the hearing of the person who seeks it ? This doesn't apply to the introduction of dancing partners, because the

lady in that case need not continue the acquaintance if she doesn't wish to.

Being Introduced

So far you have done all the introducing, but
there's the being-introduced side to consider as
well. This is quite simple, but it will give you
confidence and poise if you are quite sure beforehand when you should take the initiative and
when leave it to the other.

The query " May I introduce . . . " is purely
formal, and doesn't require any answer. The
correct way to acknowledge an introduction is
with a bow and a pleasant smile : if you like,
you may say " How-d'you-do ? " but no other
remark is expected. To shake hands is unnecessary, although when it seems kindly to do
so, the woman to whom the introduction is made
may offer her hand. And this brings us to the
two simple rules for the introduced.

(1) When a man and woman are introduced,
the woman takes the initiative. She may shake
hands, but the man must never make the first
move to do so. And if she is seated at the time,
she should not get up when the introduction is
made.

(2) When you are introduced to another

B

woman, it is her privilege to take the lead. Equally, when anyone is introduced to you, it is your place to open any conversation. Don't mention the weather if you can help it, but remember that it is better to comment on the superfluous rainfall than to leave an awkward pause.

Apply the same rules to following up an introduction. If a man has been introduced to you at a dance or dinner party, you are not bound to recognize him the next time you meet if you would rather not continue the acquaintance. On the other hand, it would be discourteous to ignore him completely unless you had very serious reason for doing so, and it is perfectly simple to give the formal bow due to a slight acquaintance without encouraging friendship. Don't make the mistake of waiting for him to give the first sign of recognition, because it would be a grave breach of good manners if he did. He expects you to make the first move.

When another woman has been introduced to you, it is equally important that you should take the next step if you'd like to become more friendly with her. When *you* have been introduced, wait for the other woman to speak first the next time you meet, and don't make any attempt to follow up the introduction if she doesn't.

Letters of Introduction

There's another form of introduction to consider : that made by letter. A friend, say, is going to live near another of your friends, and you would like them to know one another. So you give her a letter of introduction. (Be discreet, by the way, in offering such a letter : you should be reasonably certain that the two introduced will find one another pleasant and interesting acquaintances. Never write one just because you happen to know someone living in the place to which your friend is going.)

Write the letter briefly, but mention any point of interest the friends may have in common. For instance :

    " DEAR MISS BROWNE,

        " This letter is to introduce my friend, Mrs. Robinson, who is coming to live in your neighbourhood. Like you, she is an enthusiastic badminton player, and for two years has been the very able and popular secretary of the badminton club here. I am sure you will get on exceedingly well together."

Don't add any personal news to such a letter, and *don't seal the envelope into which you put it.* Simply write the address on this: Mrs. Robinson will fasten it up before it goes to Miss Browne.

She should not hand it to her personally, but leave it at her house, together with her own visiting card.

If the introduction were to a man, she should send it by post, enclosing it, with her visiting card, in another envelope.

When a letter of introduction is presented to you, it must be acknowledged at once. If possible, call the very next day on the lady who has left it, and if for any urgent reason you cannot make such a call within three or four days, write to her, explaining the reason. When you call, you should invite her to tea or to luncheon, as you prefer. And don't forget that it is courteous to send a little note of acknowledgment to the writer of the letter as well, will you?

If a letter of introduction is presented by a man, however, don't break the definite rule that a woman does not call upon a man: you should simply write a pleasant little note, extending an invitation to your house. Or, if you are married, and the introduction is to your husband as well as yourself, your husband may call and give the invitation personally.

CHAPTER II

VISITING CARDS AND THEIR USES

THE very first rule about visiting cards is that you should have the right kind of cards to leave.

No matter if you always know exactly when to leave two cards, or three, or one, as the case may be, your knowledge of the " right thing to do " will be judged by the correctness, or otherwise, of your visiting cards. So let us consider this point thoroughly before going into the matter of when and how to leave them.

Luckily, the rules about what is correct and what isn't are quite definite. First and foremost, the card *must* be plain white and of good quality, with square corners. Don't let anyone persuade you that gilt edges, or deckle edges, or rounded corners, or tinted cards are the newest and latest thing : all such variations are in distinctly bad taste. Equally to be avoided is any kind of elaborate lettering. If you're wise you will go to a really good stationer for them : " cheap " cards nearly always look cheap.

The correct size for a lady's visiting card is 3¼ inches in length by 2¼ inches deep. If you are married, you will need your husband's card to leave with your own : these must be 3 inches long by 1¼ inches deep. The name and address, in either case, should be engraved in black.

When you order your cards, there is one thing you must be *very* clear about. The name and address are not to be printed, but *engraved*. This means that the lettering will be copperplate, looking as though written on the card. As a matter of fact, it is actually hand-written on the copperplate from which the impression on each card is taken ; hence its name.

On printed cards, no matter how cleverly they imitate copperplate, you'll see a space between each letter, because they are printed from type, just as reading matter is. These printed cards are decidedly cheaper than engraved ones, but it is a serious error of taste to use them for visiting cards. Once the copperplate is engraved, furthermore, it can be used again and again when new cards are needed, so that the next ones you have will be much cheaper than the first.

The name must be in the centre of the card, and the address in the lower left-hand corner in smaller lettering than the name.

Now for the wording on the card, because there are very definite rules about this, too. It is most important that you should have " Mrs." or " Miss " before your name : it is quite incorrect to have only the Christian name and surname. A married woman uses her husband's Christian name as well as her surname, thus : " Mrs. John Hascombe " . . . never just " Mrs. Hascombe."

Whether the bachelor girl uses her Christian name depends on whether she is the eldest daughter or a younger one. An only girl, or the eldest of a family, wouldn't put it : her card would state simply : " Miss Kent ", with her address in the lower left corner. But a younger daughter, even if living away from home, would put " Miss Sheila Kent ". Girls who are living at home with their parents usually have their names on their mother's cards, just under her name.

If you are married, remember that it is just as important to have your husband's card perfectly correct as your own, since you will be leaving his with yours.

The designation " Mr. " should always be

placed before the Christian name and surname. " Mr. John Hascombe " is the correct form, unless he should be a clergyman, a doctor of medicine, or of naval or military rank. In such cases the name would be printed like this : Rev. James Turnbull: Dr. Marcus West: Lieut. Frank Martin, R.N. (a Lieutenant in the Army, as you know, is just " Mr." So-and-So): Major Alan Ward.

Orders and decorations must not be mentioned on visiting cards. No matter how many decorations Major Ward is entitled to, for instance : even if he be V.C. and D.S.O., he must not add these letters after his name on a visiting card. Neither should Orders of any kind be given.

It is equally incorrect, socially, to put one's telephone number on a visiting card. Illogical, perhaps, when we give the telephone number on our notepaper; still, it remains one of the things that " aren't done." You can, nevertheless, scribble your telephone number down in pencil when leaving a card on anybody or giving one to a friend.

Leaving Cards

Many people think of card-leaving and calling as very much the same thing. But they aren't, really. As a matter of fact, one usually leaves cards *instead* of calling. There is just one occasion when the two things go together, and that is when paying or returning a first call.

It is only the married woman who has to deal with the " how many ? " complication when leaving cards, and then it is her husband's cards, not her own, which she worries about.

Now, don't think of cards : think of husbands ! Strictly speaking, your husband, not his card, should go calling with you. As he doubtless has more urgent duties claiming him in the City, you take his visiting card along with you to represent him, and at the end of your call, leave it for your hostess.

If your hostess be married, you leave another of your husband's cards for her husband. Thus, you see, the two cards you leave for your husband are *instead* of the calls he should have paid your hostess and her husband.

Suppose your husband went with you in person to pay that call, and your host were at home, as well as his wife, you would *not* leave your husband's cards. The actual call being paid, you see, there is no need for a substitute. If the hostess only were at home, your husband would leave a card for the absent host, to represent a call on him.

If you are calling on a widow or an unmarried woman, naturally you leave only *one* of your husband's cards (representing his call upon her) since there is no husband for him to call upon.

A woman who keeps house for a bachelor brother, or a widow living with a grown-up unmarried son, may leave his cards with her own exactly as a woman would leave her husband's visiting cards. Cards may be left upon the man of the house, in such cases, as they would be for a husband.

As a woman never calls upon a man except on business, naturally she never leaves her card upon one, either, so it makes no difference to the number of your own cards whether your host be at home or not. For the same reason a widow or a bachelor girl simply leaves one card, whether her hostess be married or single.

The one time when calling and card-leaving go together is when a first call is being paid or returned. Your card then tells your hostess who you are and gives her your address. But the next time you call you don't leave your card : simply leave your husband's card (or cards, as the case may be) as you did the first time.

Nevertheless, don't go calling without your cards, for if the lady of the house happens not to be at home, then you leave your card with your husband's . . . again it is used *instead* of a call.

An Important Distinction

There is another quite important distinction between calling ‚and leaving cards. Let's suppose that you are a newcomer to a neighbourhood, and that one of the older residents leaves cards upon you, but does not ask whether you are at home. This doesn't constitute a call : she merely wishes to be civil, without pursuing the acquaintance further. You, in return, must simply leave cards upon her.

When leaving cards, you do not ask : " Is Mrs. Kent at home ? " as you would if paying a call, wishing to see the lady of the house. You just hand your card (or cards) to the servant who answers the door, saying : " Please give my card to Mrs. Kent."

Do this, too, if you in your turn wish simply to be polite to a newcomer without encouraging an acquaintance.

You must remember, though, that if Mrs. Kent has asked if you were at home, and left cards because you happened to be out at the time, you should treat this visit as a call, and when you return it, ask whether she is at home. (You'll understand from this that it is very important, if you have an inexperienced maid, to impress upon her that she should notice particularly whether a caller enquires for you, or simply leaves her card.)

If your hostess be at home, *never send in your card by the maid :* you leave it in the hall at the end of your visit.

It is correct to leave cards on your hostess, and not to pay a call, after you have been to a dance, concert, amateur theatricals, or a reception. (After a dinner party it is usual to call upon one's hostess.) This should be done within a week of the entertainment. . . . and remember that it is just as important to leave cards even though you had to decline the invitation. When, as so often happens nowadays, the entertaining is done at an hotel or public rooms, some people think it unnecessary to leave cards afterwards, but it is much more gracious to do so.

Cards must always be left *in the afternoon*

and never before 8 o'clock: it is a serious mistake to leave them at any other time in the day, except when you are enquiring after some-one who is ill. In the latter case you may write a brief message on your card, or simply " To enquire," and hand it to the maid for the invalid.

Should anyone leave on you her card with the letters " P.P.C." written in the lower right-hand corner, this means that she is leaving the neighbourhood shortly, either permanently or for a long absence. The letters stand for the French words " *Pour prendre congé* " . . . to take leave. It is correct to leave these " fare-well " cards within a week of going away.

CHAPTER III

ON CALLS AND CALLING

Call when you're called upon is a safe guide for the newcomer or the newly-married. In fact, it is a very hard-and-fast rule, and although it may seem hard when you are in a strange place and know nobody, you must wait until the older residents call upon you before you may visit them, or make a move towards getting to know them.

But once anyone has called, make a point of returning the call within ten days, or a fortnight at very most.

Four o'clock is a very good time for paying a call, although any time between 3.30 and 5.30 is permissible. No calls of any kind should be made earlier or later than this.

Before you go, put ready in your card-case just the cards you'll need, so that you can slip them out easily at the end of your call.

When you arrive at the house, enquire " Is Mrs. Blank at home ? " If she is, you will be invited in, and the maid will ask for your name. *Don't give her your card :* this is only done when you call on business. Pronounce your name distinctly, so that she can repeat it when she shows you into the drawing-room.

(It's best, by the way, not to choose a wet day for a formal call, but if the weather conspires against you, and you have with you an umbrella, wet or dry, leave it in the hall.)

If your hostess isn't already in the room, sit down in a comfortable chair while you wait for her . . . and NOT nervously on the edge of it, please . . . but don't choose the chair nearest the door.

Rise immediately when your hostess comes in : she will, of course, shake hands with you. Then you may take your seat again without waiting to be asked to.

Keep the conversation on general topics : don't volunteer copious information about your own affairs, or put questions which suggest curiosity about your hostess and her concerns.

A first call should only last fifteen to twenty minutes. It isn't necessary for the hostess to offer tea at a first call, nor for you to accept it, if offered, but if there are other visitors already there, taking tea, the natural and graceful thing would be for you to have tea, too.

There's no need for you to stay until other guests make a move to go. At the end of a quarter of an hour or so, when there is a convenient break in the general conversation, rise quietly, shake hands with your hostess (who will rise when you do) and say good-bye.

You need not shake hands with anyone else : a bow and a pleasant smile are sufficient. If you are the only visitor your hostess will probably see you to the door herself.

Anyhow, as you pass through the hall on your way out, leave your cards. Do not put them in the card tray, or hand them to the maid, but lay them down on the hall table.

After this, whether the acquaintance shall develop or not rests with the one who called first. Once you have returned her call it is up to her to pay the next one, and you must not call upon her a second time unless she does, or sends you an invitation.

If, when you return a call and ask for Mrs. Blank, the maid says she is not at home, simply hand her your cards for her mistress. This fulfils your obligation, and you should not call again until she has been to see you once more.

c

Other Calls

Who calls first when neither is a newcomer?
It may quite easily happen that two people
who have lived a long time in the same neighbourhood may meet socially for the first time at
a mutual friend's house, and would like to know
one another better. Who makes the first move?

If there be any difference in age or rank, or
one is married and the other not, this can be
decided according to the introduction. Suppose,
for example, another woman is introduced to
you, it is your place to suggest calling upon her.
Or you might say: " I do wish you would come
to see me. I am always in on Tuesday after-
noons . . . " or whatever time you are likely
to be in. You could give her your visiting card,
at the same time, so that she will know where
to find you.

But when you are the one introduced, it rests
with the other to call upon you first, or to
suggest it.

When there's little to choose between the two
in age or social position, either may take the
initiative. If the first call were returned by
cards being left, this would mean that the other
didn't wish the acquaintance to go any further,
and the matter should rest there.

A woman should never call upon a man, except on business matters. Then she would .send in her card to him by the servant. Such calls should be brief, and the conversation strictly to the point.

Nowadays calling and card-leaving are much more informal than they used to be, and in many places cards are dispensed with altogether. If you should find, in a new neighbourhood, that the calls paid on you are friendly and informal, and that nobody leaves cards, pay your return calls in the same spirit, and leave your card-case at home.

CHAPTER IV

AFTERNOON PARTIES

THERE are two simple ways of entertaining in the afternoon: you may give an informal At Home or an afternoon tea.

For the At Home, you would send cards to all the people on your calling list, to let them know that you will be At Home on a certain date. Use your ordinary visiting cards, writing both day and date immediately under your name: " At Home, Thursday, May 12th."

You need not specify the time, because it is generally understood that tea is served at about 4.80 on these occasions. These cards may be sent out by post (without any covering note, of course): if it be more convenient to leave them by hand, don't forget to enclose each in a small envelope of good quality. It isn't necessary for these invitations to be answered, so you will have to guess at the number of guests to be prepared for.

To an afternoon tea you would invite a

definite number of your friends . . . not more than your drawing-room will take comfortably. It's better to give two small tea parties than a single cramped one. (And don't, by the way, invite to a small party two people whom you know not to be on friendly terms. At a large party it doesn't matter so much, for they need have nothing to do with one another.)

Cards are not used for these invitations. You just write an informal little note, or give the invitation personally or by telephone. Such a note must be answered.

The procedure at either of these parties is the same. Remember that the " before " and " after " of your party are almost as important as the entertainment itself, and make sure that your maid understands how to show your guests in and out correctly.

A guest coming by invitation to afternoon tea doesn't enquire if the mistress of the house is at home, but walks in when the door is opened. The maid should take from her any wrap she wishes to leave in the hall, or her umbrella, and lead the way to the drawing-room. But before opening the door she should ask : " What name, please ? " Then, having opened the door, standing aside for the visitor to enter, she should repeat the name clearly enough for you to hear. She then closes the door quietly.

The maid must know how to show visitors out again nicely, too. She should listen for the drawing-room bell, which you will ring when a visitor rises to go. She will then be in the hall when the visitor comes out of the room, ready to help her on with her wraps, or to hand her umbrella to her. And *do* impress upon her not to shut the front door the moment the visitor is through it, but to wait until the latter is outside the gate, or a few steps down the street.

Tea should be placed ready in the drawing-room, but the tea itself, naturally, isn't made until the guests have arrived. If one or two are much later than the others, you need not wait for them.

The ideal plan is to have a small spirit lamp on the tea-table, so that you can make tea yourself. This ensures it being fresh and really hot. When there is quite a gap between the making of tea and the arrival of the later visitors, as there is likely to be at an At Home, fresh tea should be made for the late-comers, but this must be done without any " fussing." Instruct the maid beforehand that when she has shown the late-comers into the drawing-room, she should bring in fresh tea from the kitchen as quickly as possible. She should have plenty of boiling water in readiness.

Don't feel that you must have an elaborate display of cakes, or very rich ones. It is much more important to have excellent and very hot tea, and nicely cut bread-and-butter, scones, or small sandwiches. Besides these, a few *petits fours* or simple small cakes and a plate of cut cake will be ample. Jammy or stickily-iced things are undesirable, however attractive they may look.

When a guest rises to leave, you will rise, too, but you do not go to the door with her so long as other guests are present. (Don't forget to ring the bell warning the maid to be in the hall, will you ?)

If the man of the house should be present at an afternoon party, or one of the sons of the family, he would escort the visitor to the front door, and there would be no need for the maid to come out to the hall.

A Bridge Party

For an afternoon bridge party you would send out invitations just as for afternoon tea, but would mention, in this case, the time that the party begins . . . about 3.30 is the most usual hour. Have tea at 4.30 or a little later : it is better, if possible, to have this served in another room, so that you needn't disturb the tables.

Engraved invitation cards are sent out for a large and formal At Home where music or some special entertainment is provided.

CHAPTER V

INVITATIONS

THE friendly note is the most general form of invitation, and is used for all informal occasions . . . a little dinner, a luncheon party, a small At Home, or a garden party.

But, remember, it must be a note, not a letter. Use good stationery, of ordinary correspondence size. Word the note quite simply, and be sure that you specify the time, day, and date clearly. A " little dinner " invitation, for example, might be worded like this :

" DEAR MRS. BLAKE,

" We should be so pleased if you and Mr. Blake would dine with us on Thursday, the 7th, at half-past seven.

" Yours sincerely,"

(You'll notice that the husband should be referred to by name, not as " your husband.")

For a luncheon or afternoon party you would begin : " *I* should be," etc., instead of " *We* should . . . " Only dinner and wedding invitations are given in the names of both wife and husband.

When you receive such a note, you answer it by a note written in the first person. And always repeat the day, date and time, whether you refuse or accept the invitation. It prevents those unfortunate misunderstandings about dates that sometimes happen. For instance :

" Thank you very much for your kind invitation for Thursday, the 7th. My husband and I will be delighted to dine with you that evening at 7.30."

Or :

" We are so sorry that we cannot accept it as we have already promised to join a theatre party that evening."

When you have to decline an invitation, either formal or informal, it's much more gracious to mention the reason than to say " owing to a previous engagement."

Only when a dinner party is large and formal are invitation cards sent out. These must be engraved : any first-class stationer knows the correct wording to be used. Formal invitations are never sent for a luncheon party, no matter how many guests there are.

For a dance, engraved At Home cards are used, the lettering in copperplate script, rather larger than on visiting cards. The correct form is :

Mrs. Wynston

At Home

Wednesday, 15th June

Dancing   R.S.V.P.

9 o'clock.   24 Trevor Gardens, S.W.

The names of the people invited are written along the top left-hand corner of the card. When sending dance invitations to a family, sons of the house should each have a separate invitation, although the daughters' names may be written under those of their parents.

If you were giving a formal afternoon party, with music or some other attraction, or a *thé dansant*, you would use the same kind of card as for a dance, except that you'd change the wording in the lower left-hand corner to :

Music (or *Thé Dansant*)

4.30–7

When writing your notes of invitation to a garden party, it is well to mention whether tennis or any other game will be a feature of the afternoon. Guests at a garden party wear their very smartest frocks and hats, and probably carry parasols, but if the tennis players among them know that the tennis court will be in play, they will put on their tennis frocks or flannels, and bring their racquets with them.

Answers to all formal invitations must be in the third person :

" Mr. and Mrs. Dugdale accept with pleasure Mrs. Wynston's kind invitation for Wednesday, June 15th, at nine o'clock."

Do be careful to avoid that very frequent mistake, of writing " *will be* " pleased to accept. You are referring, remember, to the pleasure you feel at the moment of accepting, not to some future pleasure.

Never answer an informal note in the third person.

When the letters R.S.V.P. are not on an invitation card, an answer is neither expected nor necessary, but when they are, it is essential that a reply be sent . . . and PROMPTLY.

CHAPTER VI

AT A DINNER PARTY

THE most vital point of etiquette concerning a dinner party is over and out of the way before the dinner begins. It's this : *Be punctual.*

It is the height of bad manners to arrive even a few minutes after the time mentioned in the invitation. On the other hand, one should never arrive too soon . . . say, ten minutes before time. Do everything possible to reach the house or restaurant where you are dining about three or four minutes ahead of the stated time.

Arriving, you need not ask whether your hostess be at home : you will be expected to walk in. A servant may perhaps take your wraps from you in the hall, or you may be shown up to a room where you will leave them.

If a man accompanies you to the dinner party, he will wait for you in the hall when he has disposed of his own hat and coat, and you will go together to the drawing-room.

The servant will ask your name, so that she can announce it when she opens the drawing-room door. Be sure to pronounce it clearly, so that she may repeat it correctly.

When you have an escort, remember that *you* must go in first, the man following you. (If another woman is with you, the married or the elder woman goes first.) Greet your hostess before you pay any attention to anybody else, and then your host. At an informal party you will probably know the other guests : if you don't, your hostess will doubtless make one or two introductions. But at a large dinner party, don't feel slighted if you aren't introduced to guests whom you don't know, as it isn't considered necessary to make introductions all round on these occasions. If your dinner partner happen to be a stranger, he will be introduced to you, of course.

Don't linger talking to your host and hostess if other guests are present or arriving. Pass on after greeting them, and find a seat : your escort remains standing, as all the men will.

This interval before dinner is always the most difficult time of all for the hostess : the ideal guest does her best to help by chatting pleasantly to her neighbour.

The going-in-to-dinner part is very simple, because your dinner partner takes charge of you. He will offer you his right arm to lead you into the dining-room, but if a narrow passage or doorway makes single file more convenient, you go first, always.

It's up to your partner to find your places at the table, and then to pull out your chair for you, unless a servant is ready to do this. Never make a move to pull it out for yourself. You take your seat at once, though your partner mustn't take his until the hostess is seated. He will sit at your left hand.

Lift your roll from the table napkin before you, put it at the left side, unfold the napkin, and lay it across your lap. (If gloves are worn, take them off as soon as you have moved the table napkin, not before, so that the place is clear for the soup plate to be placed before you.)

The question of " which knife and fork ? " often perplexes the novice at a dinner of many courses : just remember that these are so laid at your place that you take them up in their order, beginning from the outside. Remember that it is perfectly correct to refuse a course that you don't want, and to refuse wine. If you do not care for wine, you will probably be offered mineral water.

During dinner don't give all your attention to your partner : you should talk occasionally to the man on your right hand. This leaves your partner free, too, to converse with the lady on his left now and again.

When the dessert is over, all you have to do, unless you are the guest of honour, taken in to dinner by your host, is to rise when the others do. The guest of honour, however, must watch, without seeming to do so, for the hostess to look in her direction and give the slight bow which is the signal for rising.

The most usual time to leave a dinner party is from 10.30 to 11 o'clock ; but here, again, you can wait until someone else makes a move to go. Should you have some special reason for leaving earlier than the others, there is no reason why you should not be the first to go, however.

Bid your host and hostess good-bye (not forgetting some little phrase of appreciation, such as " We have had such a delightful evening ") : there is no need to shake hands with any of the guests, or to give more than a bow and smile to those nearest you.

It is not only unnecessary but incorrect for a guest to tip any servant at a private dinner party.

At a Public Dinner

The etiquette for a public dinner is practically the same as for a private one. The invitation should be answered with equal promptness, and in the third person.

When you arrive at the restaurant or hotel where the dinner is to be held, go directly to the cloak-room, and leave your wraps there. (Full evening dress is worn on these occasions.) An attendant will be waiting to ask your name before you go into the reception room : as he is certain to announce it loudly, take care that you give it so distinctly that he can make no mistake.

In the reception room you will find the chairman and committee waiting for their guests : shake hands with the chairman, but not with the others. A bow that will include them all is sufficient. Then pass on to where the other guests are waiting.

If you are by yourself, this is a good time to study the plan of the tables, to find out where you are to sit. Sometimes the guests are handed

D

a card showing the arrangement of the tables : at others, a large chart is hung in some conspicuous place.

No special precedence is observed in going in to dinner. The chairman and his principal guests lead the way, while the rest follow quietly in any order convenient.

When the toast of " *The King* " is announced, rise to your feet with the other guests, and with your right hand lift your wine-glass, untouched, to the level of your eyes. Say " The King ! " looking at your glass as you do so, then drink your wine.

When dinner is over, no leave-taking is necessary. Simply collect your wraps from the cloak-room as soon as you all rise from the table, and go.

You need have no worry about tips. A woman is not expected to give any at a public dinner, except to the cloak-room attendant.

CHAPTER VII

GIVING A LITTLE DINNER PARTY

WHEN you plan a little dinner, remember that there isn't the ghost of a rule in etiquette that a dinner should be elaborate, or consist of so many courses, or be served according to a set ritual. A " soup, joint and sweet " dinner is every bit as correct as a seven-course meal . . . provided that it conform to three rules which apply to all dinner parties : that whatever is served shall be cooked as perfectly as possible ; that it shall be nicely served ; that the guests shall be congenial.

Arrange your menu according to your means . . . your " means " including the capabilities of the cook, whoever she be, and the service available. Fortunately for the average house-wife elaborate dishes and many courses are much oftener the exception than the rule nowadays.

For a formal dinner, all carving is done at a side-table, and everything is served from this, too. A dinner of this kind should only be attempted where there are two servants to attend to the carving and waiting. At such a meal the menu might consist of fruit cocktail or grape-fruit (or oysters in season); soup; fish; either cutlets, joint or game; a sweet and a savoury; dessert and coffee. Or it might start with consommé, and include an entrée between the fish and game.

Where there is but one maid to do the waiting, serving and carving should be done by host and hostess at the table. Soup and sweets are served by the hostess, and the carving is done by the host: either may serve the fish course. To simplify service, the first course, whether it be grape-fruit, oysters or the soup, may be placed ready on the table before the guests enter.

But don't be prevented from giving a little dinner because you can't trust your maid to wait expertly at the table. Let her simply place the dish to be served, with the plates, before host or hostess, as the case may be, and let the server hand the plates to the guests, beginning always with the lady on the host's right hand. Vegetables, sauces, gravy and so on should be placed on the table for the guests themselves to pass round. The host will be responsible for pouring wine or mineral waters.

If you have no maid at all, plan your dishes so that they can be served up easily . . . fish cooked in individual marmites, *au gratin* fashion, or so that no separate sauce is needed; the meat or game prepared *en casserole* to make dishing up unnecessary, and so on. Serve the soup in individual bowls, standing these, each in its soup plate, at the guests' places, before you summon them to dinner. Instead of dessert, little dishes of bon-bons may be placed on the table, to be handed round with the after-dinner coffee, which it is now quite usual for the hostess to make at the table.

In planning your dinner table, seat the most important lady at the host's right hand, with the one next in rank at his left. The chief man sits at his hostess's left hand, the second in importance at her right. In placing the remaining guests, bear in mind that husband and wife should not be sent in together, nor two members of the same family.

The host, when dinner is announced, leads the way to the dining-room with his partner, and the hostess comes last, with hers. A bachelor girl giving a little dinner party should waive this rule, and lead the way.

At a small dinner, where there are no place-cards on the table . . . these are quite unnecessary when there are only six or eight guests . . . the host should tell the guests where to sit. He must remain standing until all his guests are seated. You should sit down as soon as the other women are seated, because your men guests will remain standing as long as you do.

When menu cards are provided, they are written out by the hostess, but these are unnecessary for a small party. If you are giving a more formal dinner, and wish to use them, remember that the items are usually given their French names (which you will be able to find in a good cookery book, if you don't know them), and that the vegetables, sauces, dessert and coffee are not mentioned. For example :

MENU

14th May

Consommé Printanière
Filets de Sole à la Normande
Poularde Rôti
Glace aux Pêches
Ramequins de Fromage

You know, of course, that it is your duty to

give the signal for the ladies to make a move to the drawing-room, catching the eye of the lady at the host's right hand, so that she may rise with you. The man nearest the door will open it for you to go out, and stand by it until all the ladies have passed through.

Laying the Table

The correct laying of the dinner table is as important as the excellent cooking of the dishes to be served on it. The table linen . . . whether you use a cloth or mats . . . must be smooth and spotless, the silver and glass polished to sparkling, knives and forks symmetrically placed, salt and pepper containers freshly filled.

Whether you use mats on a polished table, or a white tablecloth, is a matter of personal taste. Fashions change, too, so that it is impossible to lay down a definite rule that will hold good from season to season. The modern feeling is definitely towards simplicity, in table appointments, decoration, lighting, as well as in the menu, and any suspicion of ostentation is regarded as bad taste.

Silver and cutlery are arranged in the order in which they will be used : the soup spoon on the extreme right, the fish knife next to it (on the left), the meat knife to the left of that, and the corresponding forks placed in the same order on the left of the cover. The entrée fork, when this is necessary, comes between the fish and meat forks. The spoon and fork for the sweet are usually placed at the top, the spoon above the fork, with its handle to the right, the fork handle to the left. The dessert knife and fork come to the table on the dessert plate, when that course is served.

Don't make the mistake of laying cutlery for a course that will not be given, as is sometimes done. Be careful that everything necessary for the dishes provided is in its place, but nothing else.

Salt and pepper should be provided for each two diners, and be placed between them. Small plates for bread or rolls may or may not be provided, according to your preference. Table napkins must be folded as simply as possible: a dinner roll or neat square of bread is placed in each. Glasses are set according to the wines to be offered : at a formal party tumblers are in readiness on the sideboard for those preferring plain water, but at a small party a tumbler is set with the wine glasses.

When dishes are to be handed round by the

maid, an adequate supply of serving spoons, sauce-ladles and so on must be laid out ready on the sideboard, with extra rolls, water for those who prefer it, and so on. In any case the dessert plates should be placed ready on a side table, dessert knife and fork laid on each. If finger bowls be used, place one on each plate, a small doily under it, and the knife and fork at either side. The bowl should be not more than half-filled with water.

When serving and carving are to be done by host and hostess at the table, the necessary knives, forks and spoons should be placed on either side of their covers. Spoons for vegetables, when these are passed round by the guests, are placed at the corners of the table, about ten inches from it, with their bowls pointed in opposite directions.

The first course, if it be grape-fruit, melon, oysters or soup, may be placed ready at each cover when the diners enter. In such a case the soup should be served in covered marmites, or little bowls, to keep it really hot.

The maid removes the plates as each guest finishes : the host and hostess make a point of finishing last.

When soup is served from a tureen, the maid

should place this and the plates before the
hostess, then stand at her left, ready to take
each plate as filled, and place it before a guest,
always from the left side. It is correct to serve
first the lady on the host's right hand, then
the lady on his left, and after that each guest
in turn right round the table. The maid removes the tureen to the sideboard as soon as
she has handed the last soup plate, as second
helpings of soup are not offered. She should
then pour out the wine served with this course :
to do this, she stands at the right hand of the
diner, the glasses being placed at that side.
Wine glasses should be filled to within about
half an inch of the brim. If a guest prefers water
or lemonade, this is poured into a tumbler to within an inch and a half, or thereabouts, of the brim.

The soup plates are removed to the sideboard
one (or, if convenient, two) at a time : the
piling together of used plates must always be
done at the sideboard, and never at the table.
The fish is then placed before host or hostess,
as arranged, and is handed by the maid in the
same way as the soup, but if there is an accompanying sauce, she should carry this in her left
hand, so that guests may help themselves when
the fish is handed to them.

The joint or game course is served likewise, the maid handing gravy, sauce or a vegetable at the same time as the plate of meat, bringing any second vegetable round after all the plates have been handed. Fish and joint may be left before the server until the guests have been offered a second helping. In taking away the joint, carving knife and fork should be removed first, and not left on the dish.

The servant should watch to see whether guests need more bread, sauce, vegetables and so on, and keep them supplied. She may also attend to the re-filling of the wine glasses, or the host may prefer to look after this himself.

The hostess serves the sweets, but if there is a savoury, this is usually handed. Hot plates are first put round before the diners, then the dish containing the savoury . . . invariably served in small individual portions . . . is handed.

Before dessert is served, the table should be cleared of everything not needed for that course : salt (unless dessert includes nuts), pepper, glasses, plates, knives and forks. These must be removed on a small tray, and the crumbs taken up from cloth or polished table :

it is considered better to use a table-napkin and plate than a brush-and-crumb tray for this. The dessert plates with finger bowls are placed before the diners, and dessert handed.

When coffee is served in the dining-room, it may be made by the hostess, or brought in ready poured out (the cups three-quarters filled), cream and sugar being handed with them. After-dinner coffee *must* be boiling hot. Cigarettes are handed so that the ladies may smoke with their coffee. If you prefer, have coffee brought into the drawing-room instead, the cups being handed round on a tray, with cream and sugar.

At a small dinner party it is unnecessary to give many wines. If it's a rather special and somewhat formal party, you might serve sherry with the soup, and provide white wine and claret to follow, allowing the guests to choose between white wine and red. There should be whisky-and-soda, and lemonade or mineral water, for those who prefer these to wine. Port is served with dessert. But for just a friendly party it is quite enough to give either a good white wine or Burgundy or claret (*not* all three) with the whisky and mineral water alternatives as before. Port with dessert is entirely optional.

CHAPTER VIII

TABLE ETIQUETTE

WHEN you sit down to a dinner or luncheon of many courses, don't be alarmed at the number of knives and forks laid at your place, and start wondering which you use, and when! You'll only be served with one course at a time, and the cutlery is so arranged that you take the outermost each time.

For *hors d'œuvres,* . . . those fascinating appetite-tempters like anchovies, Russian salad, sardines, smoked herring and the like . . . the appropriate silver knife and fork are often placed on the plate. Olives generally come on with this course, but to these you help yourself with your fingers, one at a time, and eat with your fingers, too. When caviar is served, toast comes too, and a special little knife. Press one or two of the balls on a corner of toast, then bite off that portion. When caviar is served *on* toast, eat this with knife and fork.

Grape-fruit or melon are often served instead

of *hors d'œuvres*. You'll find the sections of grape-fruit all cut away from the rind and divided, ready for you, and you take them one at a time with the spoon provided : sometimes a dessert spoon, but generally a smaller one. You may steady the grape-fruit holder with your left hand. Melon is eaten with a dessert-spoon.

Oysters are another alternative for this first course. Use an oyster fork or an ordinary small dinner fork for these, taking up the oyster whole, and steadying the shell on its plate with your left hand. Cut lemon is usually handed with oysters : take a piece in your fingers, and squeeze the juice over the oysters. (Lemon handed with fish is treated in the same way.) And if you dislike oysters, or feel doubtful about your skill in eating them, you will be quite correct in refusing them.

Soup is eaten with a large spoon . . . laid at your extreme right . . . and always from the side of the spoon. If served in a cup, drink it from this. When a small marmite of soup is placed on your soup plate, take your soup direct from the marmite (this is a little casserole of earthenware) and don't empty it into the plate. You may tilt your plate slightly if you need to, but always *away* from you : don't try to scoop up the very last drop. And never break your bread or roll into your soup.

Fish knives and forks you'll recognize. Remember that whitebait must be eaten whole—that is, heads and tails included—and never more than two at a time should be taken on the fork : when they're large, only one.

Egg dishes, generally served in small individual earthenware dishes, are eaten with a fork. It is better to steady the dish with your left hand than to chase it round the plate with your fork . . . but be wary, for these dishes *should* be piping hot.

Entrées of a soft kind, such as rissoles, *pâtés*, and the like, are eaten with a large fork only : sweetbreads and cutlets need a knife as well : curry, a fork and spoon.

Joints and poultry you can easily manage. Don't start eating them before you are served with vegetables. Salad is put on the salad plate placed at your left, and you eat it from this, without transferring it to your dinner plate. Use a fork or knife and fork, as is most convenient. Cucumber is taken on the dinner plate, and eaten with a fork.

When small birds are served, such as quail or tiny pigeons, remember that you are expected to cut the meat only from the breast and the wings . . . even though this be but a mouthful. It is not correct to turn the bird over, or to try to get all the meat from the bones.

The sweet course should be eaten with a fork whenever possible : with fruit tart, or anything like that, use a dessertspoon as well. Fruit salad is eaten with a dessertspoon only.

The savoury, which is usually something small and piquant and very hot, served on toast, should be eaten with a fork only, unless a knife be absolutely necessary. At a formal dinner party the implements for sweet and savoury will probably be placed on the table when these courses come along. Ices are eaten with a small spoon.

With dessert will come finger bowls. Lift yours off the dessert plate (and if it stands on a doily take that, too) and put it at your left side. At the end of dessert dip the tips of your fingers very lightly in the water, and *pat* them dry on your napkin. It is quite incorrect to wipe them on it.

At a dinner party where there are several wines, the question of the correct glass needn't worry you, for the servant will pour whatever wine you choose into its appropriate one.

Sherry is usually served with the soup (in a small, slim glass with a stem): Sauterne, Chablis, or other white wine with the fish. Claret or champagne may be served during the following courses: champagne glasses have a wide, rather shallow bowl on a thin stem. Port (in a small glass with a stem) is served with dessert. Liqueurs, served in tiny glasses, because they are very potent, nearly always accompany coffee, and sometimes the ices as well. A liqueur should always be taken in tiny sips.

If you are unaccustomed to wines, it is wiser to refuse them on occasions like this : you will not be in the least " odd " or incorrect. Simply say " No, thank you," when they are offered, and the butler or waiter will suggest lemonade or mineral water instead. In any case, don't " mix " your wines. Remember, if you do take wine, that your glass will be filled up again as a matter of course if you empty it, so if you don't wish for more, leave some in your glass. Do not take a long drink of any kind of wine, nor drink it quickly.

At the end of a meal crumple up your napkin lightly, and leave it on table or chair : *never* fold it.

E

Second helpings are never offered at dinner parties : when helping yourself to any dish or its accompanying sauce, take only a small portion.

If everyone else has finished their course, and you are only half-way through yours, it is much more polite to place your knife and fork together on the plate, and let it be cleared away, than to keep the others waiting while you finish.

CHAPTER IX

VISITORS AND VISITING

WHETHER you give or receive an invitation to visit, *do be definite about dates*. Mention the length of the proposed visit, as well as the date it is to begin. For instance, there can be no misunderstanding about an invitation worded on these lines :

" We shall be so pleased if you will spend the week-end after next (September 7th to 10th) with us. If you arrive on Friday evening, we shall have a nice long day for golf on Saturday. There is a train leaving Waterloo at 5.50 which will bring you here in good time for dinner."

It is much more considerate to suggest a train or a definite time for your guest to arrive, and much easier for you, as you know just when to expect her.

When you accept such an invitation, be sure to mention dates and time in your reply, like this :

" I shall be delighted to come to you on September 7th for the week-end. Thank you so much for looking up the train for me : you may expect me by the 5.50 on Friday evening."

If you are asked for " the week-end " without dates being mentioned, assume that this begins on Saturday, and that you will be expected for tea. In accepting, mention the time of your arrival ; for example :

" I find that there is a train arriving at Bishop's Moreton at 4 o'clock on Saturday afternoon, and I will arrange to come by this."

A " week-end," unless some specific arrangement has been made otherwise, should end after breakfast on the Monday morning. Look up your return train beforehand, for if on Monday morning you ask your hostess what would be a good train for you to take, politeness may prompt her to name one much later in the day than is really convenient to her. She can't very well name the earliest possible train after breakfast, which is the one you should take !

When invited for a " few days," this must be taken to mean less than a week. Be specific about the dates in your answer . . . " I should like very much to come from August 12th to 14th, if that is quite convenient to you ? "

Once dates have been arranged, do stick to them ! The guest who lightly postpones a visit at the last minute, or alters dates, is a trial to any hostess. And if you do, for some very serious reason, have to put off a visit, let your hostess know at the earliest possible moment, so that she may adjust her own plans.

It is just as important to be punctual about the time you leave as about the time you arrive. However much you are enjoying yourself, *go when you said you would*. Many hostesses urge a guest to stay on, from a sense of hospitality, but you should never do so, except in those special cases where common sense tells you you may.

Between your punctual arrival and punctual departure, please be a punctual guest . . . and you'll be a popular one. Be prompt for all meals. If your hostess doesn't tell you what the meal times are, don't be afraid to ask her. Should an excursion be arrranged, be ready for it in good time : *really* ready, so that you don't need to rush upstairs again for your bag or your hankie or your tennis racquet just as everybody is starting off.

Amuse yourself in the morning, so that your

hostess is free to look after household affairs. If she has to do a good deal of the work herself, offer to help her, but don't *insist* on helping. You can in any case give a good deal of indirect assistance by keeping your own room in perfect order, leaving the bathroom tidy after you, and so on.

Fit in cheerfully with plans made for your entertainment, even if you don't care for picnics and clock golf is your weakest point. But when asked to make a choice, *make it*. A guest who perpetually " doesn't mind " what she does is irritating in the extreme.

What to take with you depends so much on where and when you are going, and what you are going to do. Speaking generally, sports clothes, practical shoes and stockings, with rain coat and rain-resisting hat, belong to the country outfit . . . but don't assume that your second best dinner frock is " good enough " to accompany them. People dance in the country as well as in the town nowadays. For town you will need especially chic footwear and smarter day frocks and hats.

But wherever you are going, see that your toilet accessories are irreproachable and neatly packed, and be supplied with plenty of stockings, handkerchiefs, underwear and a dressing-gown that would make you greet a fire-alarm with equanimity.

Tips ! Well, here's a tip about them. *Don't try to make them too lavish.* That's the mistake many inexperienced girls make, because they are terrified of giving too little. For a week's stay, or part of a week, it is ample for a woman to give the housemaid half-a-crown, and perfectly correct to give less, according to her means. If the maid has given any special help to the guest, the tip might be 3s. 6d.

A woman, remember, is not expected to tip men-servants, except the chauffeur : if he has taken her to and from the station, and driven her about during the visit, she may give him half-a-crown.

Do give your tip personally, with a pleasant word of thanks. You can present the maid's tip when she brings your early morning tea on the last morning : it is so much more gracious than leaving it behind in one's room.

When you get home, write *at once* to your hostess to let her know how much you have enjoyed your visit, and to thank her. This is just as important after a week-end as after a long visit.

CHAPTER X

ON BEING ENTERTAINED

It is every whit as important to be punctual when you are invited out to a restaurant or theatre, as when you go to a private house. If you are being entertained by a man, don't be deluded by the old-fashioned theory that it is " good to keep him waiting." It isn't : it is merely ill-bred.

Certainly you may allow yourself five minutes' grace, and you should try to avoid arriving before the appointed time, but to keep your escort hanging about just for the sake of it is an exhibition of bad manners.

Never wait about *outside* a theatre, restaurant, concert hall, or other place of entertainment. Go directly to the entrance hall or lobby, and if you don't immediately see your host (or your party) don't stand gazing about distractedly, but walk quietly to a seat. Not even the most eager host can dissolve a traffic block, and delays will happen to the best-intentioned taxi or omnibus.

Seat yourself, if you can, where you can conveniently watch the entrance. But watch unobtrusively ; not with fixed and desperate gaze. Refrain, too, from rushing across the lobby to greet your host when he does arrive. On the other hand, even though you consider him inexcusably late, do not show your annoyance openly, nor utter loud reproaches.

Should your host, however, call for you there are one or two other little rules to bear in mind. Whether you travel by taxi, train or bus, remember that you enter the vehicle first, and that your escort alights first, so that he may help you out. When you get into a taxi, take the seat farthest from the entrance door : in a bus, the inside seat (if there be any choice !)

At your destination, walk quietly into the entrance lobby while your escort settles with the driver, if you have come by taxi. It is quite incorrect to wait beside him. (Incidentally, never linger at your escort's elbow while he settles a bill, takes theatre tickets, and so on.)

At Luncheon or Dinner

When lunching or dining at a restaurant, leave your heavy wraps or an umbrella in the ladies' cloak-room. Give them to the attendant in charge, so that you get a numbered ticket for them, otherwise you will have difficulty in claiming them again.

As you enter the restaurant . . . you will go in first . . . a waiter will come forward : with him your escort will arrange about a table, if one has not been booked beforehand. In either case the waiter will lead the way to it, and you follow him, your companion coming after you.

If it should happen that no waiter notices your entrance, and you have to walk down the room in search of a table, then your escort must precede you. At the end of a meal, however, it is always your place to make the first move towards leaving, and to walk out first.

(For this reason, if you are going on to a theatre afterwards, *you* are responsible for arriving before the curtain rises, remember, and you should allow ample time. It is both inconsiderate and discourteous to disturb those seated near you in a theatre by coming in during the first act.)

When there are two or more women in the party, a married woman takes precedence over one who is unmarried, or when both are married or both single, the elder takes the initiative. When a mother and her young daughter are out together, the younger woman should always wait for the elder to precede her.

At any restaurant meal, when you are being entertained, never give any order yourself to the waiter ; if you wish for more bread, or another lump of sugar in your coffee, for instance, let your host ask for them.

Should you unfortunately drop a fork, spoon or knife, *never pick it up*. The waiter will bring you another, and remove the dropped one.

At Theatre or Concert

The rule of " ladies first " should be waived when entering theatre or concert hall. If the man goes first, following the attendant down the aisle, he can stand aside at the end of their particular row of seats for the lady to enter first, while he gives up the tickets and buys a programme.

If you've kept your wrap with you . . . always a wise thing to do in case of draughts . . . and begin to feel too hot in it after the play has begun, slip it off your shoulders as inconspicuously as possible, so that you do not interrupt the view of those behind you. Should that tiresome " train-to-catch " cause you to leave before the end of the play, pick up your wraps and slip out as quietly as possible, with a low-spoken apology to those you have to pass: " I'm so sorry to disturb you," or something like that. It is very inconsiderate—and therefore in extremely bad taste—to put on your hat or struggle into a coat, while still in your place. If you've any impedimenta such as chocolate box, programme, gloves or umbrella to gather up, collect these quietly during the last interval, to avoid any fussing after them in the dark when it's time to go.

You wouldn't think it necessary, would you, to warn people not to rustle programmes unnecessarily, rattle chocolate boxes, or carry on a conversation, even in a whisper, while the play is going on ? But these irritating things happen over and over again, and for the offenders to plead thoughtlessness is no excuse, since good manners are based on consideration for other people.

Entertained Unawares

Hospitality may be thrust upon you unsought. You meet a friend in restaurant or tea-room, and he or she urges so pressingly that you shall have lunch or tea together that you cannot well refuse : perhaps you don't wish to. But you

do want to pay your share, if not the whole bill.
When the moment for settling comes, your
friend has an equally firm intention of paying
the whole amount.

Make your request quietly, but *don't wrangle
before the waitress.* When you are alone with
your friend afterwards pleasantly but firmly
ask to be allowed to pay your share. Courtesy
should prompt her to agree. If you have shared
an " accidental " meal, as one might call it,
with a man (on the train, for example) the best
plan is for you to ask the waiter, when he comes
to make out the bill, for separate ones.

CHAPTER XI

TRAVEL TIPS

MANY women who would like to take a " wander-holiday " or occasional short visits to new places, hesitate because they aren't used to hotels, and the thought of tips terrifies them. Yet the etiquette for both problems is very simple.

When you can, it is best to book rooms beforehand at the hotel you think of going to. If you are journeying abroad any good travel agency will recommend an hotel at the price you want to pay.

When you reach the hotel, go straight to the office to enquire about your room, whether you have booked beforehand or not. Even if you haven't, don't cling on to your luggage. Hand it over to the porter who will doubtless come forward to take it as you enter.

If your room is booked, the clerk will tell you its number, and give the key to a servant, who will take you up. Probably you will be asked to register your name in the visitors' book first :

note, by the way, that you should put " Mrs."
or " Miss," as the case may be, before your
name. (Husband and wife travelling together
don't sign separately, but register as " Mr. and
Mrs. Blank " : a man by himself simply signs
Christian name and surname.)

You'll doubtless find in your room a notice
stating the time of meals and so on : if not, you
can get all the information at the office.

When you come down to meals, or when going
out, lock your room and hand the key in at the
office, where you claim it again when you need
it. It is not wise to leave it in your door.
Should you have anything of special value with
you, hand it in at the office, to be locked up
safely for you.

As you will probably be going sight-seeing
directly after breakfast, you may come down
to that meal, if you wish, wearing your hat
ready for going out. At luncheon a hat is
generally worn. For dinner, except at a very
smart hotel where evening dress is the general
rule, a simple dinner frock is best. At the kind
of hotel where one would stay on a wandering
holiday, an afternoon dress is quite sufficient.

If you are planning an excursion which means
an early start, and you want to be called in good

time, leave instructions for this with the clerk in the office. Chambermaids are very busy people, and if you give them directions of this kind, they may be overlooked. Do the same when you are leaving, and want your luggage taken down.

A perfectly safe rule about tips is ten per cent of the bill. This is adequate for any traveller, and is recognized as quite fair by hotel servants themselves. Women aren't expected to give large tips, anyhow. How you divide the ten per cent depends entirely upon what services you have received.

If you have had all your meals in the hotel, the head waiter will expect the largest share. Give this to him at the end of your last meal there. If you have had breakfast only, in your own room, brought up by the chambermaid, give her more than you do the others.

In any case, ring for her just before you leave, and present the tip personally, with a word of thanks. Tip the hall porter as you leave, likewise the luggage porter, if he attends to your bags.

Don't wait until the last minute to settle your bill. If you are leaving early in the morning, ask for it the night before : the head waiter will get it for you, if you ask him at your last meal, or you can call at the office for it.

If you aren't leaving till late in the day, be sure to give notice *before midday* that you are going, or you will be charged for an extra day.

CHAPTER XII

ENGAGEMENTS

WHEN you get engaged to be married, don't hurry round announcing your engagement to the world in general the moment it takes place.

Your parents, and those of your fiancé, of course, should be told at once. The once-rigid rule of consulting father first is very seldom observed in these days, but the young man should at least consult him second !

Even if the girl be living away from home, and more or less independent, it is only courteous of the young man to write to him before the engagement is announced.

The young man's family should write at once to his fiancée, or call on her whenever that is possible, welcoming her into the family circle. Neither the girl nor her mother should take the first step in this matter.

A girl must never visit her fiancé's people on his invitation alone. No matter how strongly he urges that " she'll just love to have you," wait for his mother to send a definite written invitation, or to give it to you personally.

Making the acquaintance of one's future " in-laws " is often rather an ordeal, but it would be ungracious to put it off by refusing invitations to meet them. If the man's people live some distance away, and don't know the girl at all, they will probably ask her to stay with them for a few days . . . an invitation which should be accepted if it be anyhow possible.

The girl's mother will perhaps give a little dinner, or an informal evening party, inviting the family's nearest relatives, so that they may meet the young man.

When letters of felicitation begin to come in, they must be answered *at once*. Such answers are primarily to send thanks for kind wishes, and need not be long.

Mentioning felicitations, when your brother, or son, or other very near relative, becomes engaged, don't *congratulate* the girl, even though in your heart you think how lucky she is to have won Peter for a husband. Just offer your best wishes for her happiness, and let her feel in your note or your remarks a genuine welcome into your home circle.

As a general rule it is considered tactless to

" congratulate " a girl on her engagement. The young man, it is understood, is the one to be congratulated. So it is better to write " Let me wish you every possible happiness " than to say " Let me congratulate you on your engagement."

If the young man does not already know the girl's preference in the matter of stones for the engagement ring, he should certainly find out what it is before buying such an important thing.

However beautiful the ring, though, don't draw attention to it constantly by fiddling with it, or glancing at it ostentatiously.

Don't monopolize each other too much. Most of your friends, when inviting one of you to a party, will now ask the other, as well, but when one alone is invited, there is no reason why the invitation shouldn't be accepted.

CHAPTER XIII

CONCERNING WEDDINGS

ALL the invitations to a wedding are sent out by the bride's parents, even those to the bridegroom's relations and his personal friends. These invitations should go out about three weeks or a fortnight before the wedding.

So long as it is plain and simple there is no very strict rule about the type of invitation card. The invitation which is engraved on a small double sheet of very good notepaper, folding over to form its own envelope, is perhaps still the most usual, although cards with envelopes to match are allowed, too.

Any good stationer will advise you about this, but you must avoid ornamentation or elaborate lettering. Black lettering is newer than silver, but both are considered correct.

The wording is always the same for a formal invitation, and is in the third person. For example :

" *Mr. and Mrs. Foster request the pleasure of the company of Mr. and Mrs. James at the marriage of their daughter Mary to Mr. John Price at St. Mark's Church, Bayswater, on Tuesday, June 11th, at 2.30.*"

When breakfast or a reception is to be held after the wedding there should be added :

" *and afterwards at* 999 *Marlborough Gardens, S.W.*," or wherever the reception is to be held.

The address of the bride's parents should be engraved in the lower left-hand corner of the invitation, and the letters " R.S.V.P." in the right-hand corner.

When you answer such an invitation, follow the same form: " . . . accept with much pleasure So-and-so's kind invitation to the marriage of their daughter Mary to . . . " and so on, repeating all the particulars in the order in which they appear in the invitation.

If you have to decline, it is more courteous, remember, to give your reason for doing so. In either case, it is essential to answer promptly.

When a girl has no mother, invitations may be sent out by a relative, or an old friend of the family, when the same form would be used. But when she has no one to undertake this for her, the bride-elect would simply write informal little notes of invitation herself, and *not* use printed cards.

For a quiet wedding, when only a few people are to be present, informal notes are sent instead of invitation cards.

In the case of a second marriage, the bride's parents may send out the invitations, or the bride may send them herself, worded something like this :

" *The pleasure of your company is requested at the marriage of Mrs. Peter Blank to Mr. John Dash,*" etc., the particulars following in the order already given.

Wedding presents usually begin to arrive as soon as the invitations are received. There is no fixed rule about the time of sending these : some people send theirs soon after the engagement is announced. But there *is* a fixed time for acknowledging them : if possible, a cordial letter of thanks should go the same day, or the next day at latest.

When there are a great many presents, the wise bride makes a list of them, with the donors'

names, so that there may be no awkward
contretemps later on.

Publishing the Banns.

The clergyman of the church where the wedding is to take place should be consulted in
good time. Banns must be published on three
consecutive Sundays before the wedding, and
seven days' notice must be given before the
first publication. For a wedding in a Nonconformist church a " certificate of notice "
must be obtained from a superintendent
registrar of marriages : this takes three weeks
to obtain, and a week's notice must be given
beforehand. In any case, the clergyman of
one's own church will be able to give any information required.

When the wedding is a choral one, or the
church is to be decorated, the expenses for these
things are paid by the bride's parents. They are
also responsible for the carriage which takes the
bride to the church, and for the reception after
the ceremony. The guests provide their own
conveyances.

The Wedding Day

On the wedding day the first to arrive at the

church should be the tactful friend (or friends) whom you have enlisted to meet your guests and show them to their seats. They should be on duty at least three-quarters of an hour before the ceremony begins.

The guests will probably begin to arrive any time after that : they should all be in their places before the bride is due at the church. The front seats are reserved for relations and intimate friends : those of the bride sit on the left of the aisle, and of the groom on the right. The bride's mother takes the seat nearest the aisle, in the front pew. At a wedding where there is no usher, the guests should follow these rules in seating themselves : the bride's friends always on the left of the aisle, and the bridegroom's on the right.

Bridegroom and best man should take their places at the chancel steps some minutes before the bride is due. The bridesmaids should arrive well ahead of her, too, but they wait in the porch, ready to fall in behind her as she walks up the aisle on her father's right arm.

The bride takes her place at the left of the bridegroom ; at *her* left stands whoever is to give her away. The best man stands slightly behind the bridegroom, to the right.

The chief bridesmaid waits just behind the bride, a little to the left, and takes her bouquet and gloves (many modern brides dispense with gloves) before the ceremony begins. None of these attendants should follow bride and bridegroom when they move up to the altar.

After the ceremony the parents and immediate relations, such as sisters and brothers, follow the married pair to the vestry, where the register is signed. Best man and chief bridesmaid go, too; whether the other bridesmaids follow depends very much on the size of the vestry, and *should be arranged beforehand.* If they don't, they must remain in the church ready to follow bride and bridegroom down the aisle.

The best man is responsible for the payment of all fees: those to the clergyman, verger and so on, he should settle beforehand if possible.

After the register is signed, the bride takes her husband's right arm to walk down the church: the bridesmaids follow in the same order as before.

Guests should *not* step out into the aisle to waylay the couple and congratulate them:

all that should be left until the reception. They should remain in their places until relations have left the church and then follow on to the reception, if there be one.

At the house, the bride's mother should greet all the guests as they enter the drawing-room : she will stand near the door. The bride and bridegroom stand together further inside the room to receive the good wishes of their friends. Refreshments are served as soon as these greetings are over. Nowadays these refreshments are usually handed from a buffet. The formal breakfast and its accompanying formal speeches are now seldom part of a wedding entertainment.

If champagne is drunk, this is generally handed round when the bride cuts the cake, and an informal little speech may be made, proposing the health of the young couple. In response the bridegroom should make a brief speech of thanks. When the bridesmaids are toasted, the best man replies for them.

The chief bridesmaid generally slips away with the bride when she goes to change into travelling things, but the other bridesmaids remain with the guests.

When you are a guest at a wedding, make

your farewells as soon as possible after bride and bridegroom have departed : it is quite correct to leave before they go, if you wish to, and it is unnecessary to bid them good-bye if you do.

CHAPTER XIV

CHRISTENINGS

So important an event as Baby's arrival is very often announced by his parents in one or more of the daily newspapers. The wording of this paragraph varies a good deal, but the following is considered the most correct form :

Browne.—On the 10th September, at 10 West Terrace, Northbourne, the wife of James Browne, of a son.

If you are a friend of the parents, you will send a note of congratulation at once. It isn't in the least necessary to send a present of any kind, but most babies do gather quite a harvest of little welcoming gifts, which their mothers will acknowledge later on.

Baby's christening is generally regarded as quite an informal occasion as regards invitations, and any entertainment given after the ceremony. Usually only personal friends and relations are invited and the invitations given verbally, or

in the form of a brief note, worded something
like this :

" MY DEAR MRS. SMITH,

"We should be so pleased if you would be
present at St. Mark's Church next Tuesday, October
3rd, at 3 o'clock, when Baby is to be christened.
We hope that you will come back to tea with us
afterwards."

Should the christening take place at a
fashionable church, with a large number of
guests invited, printed cards of invitation might
be sent. In such case, the wording would be
in the third person.

"Mr. and Mrs. James Browne request the pleasure
of the company of Mr. and Mrs. Smith on Tuesday
afternoon, October 3rd, at 3 o'clock, at St. Mark's
Church, on the occasion of the christening of their
son, and afterwards at 10 West Terrace, Northbourne."

Any good stationer will set out the wording
in the correct form : remember that good taste
demands the utmost simplicity in lettering and
the kind of card used.

In either case, be sure that the invitations
include one to the clergyman who is to baptise
the child.

These invitations should be answered promptly

in the first or third person, according to the kind of invitation received.

If you are one of the invited, and haven't already sent Baby a present, you will probably be sending one for his christening, although acceptance of the invitation doesn't put you under any obligation to do so. Dispatch it so that it will arrive a day or so before the event, for Baby's mother may like to arrange the gifts on a small table for the guests to see. Christening presents should be acknowledged as soon as possible by the mother.

Guests should be in their places in the church a few minutes before the time mentioned on the invitation. The parents and godparents stand near the font : the guests are seated as near the font as is convenient.

A boy should have two godfathers and a godmother ; a girl, two godmothers and a godfather.

The godmother (when the baby is a girl, the principal godmother) holds the child, standing at the clergyman's left, and handing Baby to him at the right moment. If you are acting as godmother for the first time you need not feel anxious about this point, for the clergyman will take the child from you when he is ready, and hand him back to you after he is baptised.

Hold the child, by the way, so that you can most conveniently place him on the clergyman's *left* arm. If Baby has a nurse, she often holds him (as being most likely to keep him quiet and happy) just handing him to the godmother in time for her to give him, in turn, to the clergyman.

When they return to the house after the ceremony, everyone, naturally, will want to admire Baby, and handle him, too. But when you are godparent or guest on such an occasion, don't forget that the small mite has already had quite as much excitement as is good for him, if not more. So the child should be carried off to his quiet nursery as soon as the guests have had their " peep." Only the very thoughtless guest will beg for him to stay longer.

Tea after the ceremony shouldn't be an elaborate affair : provide thin bread-and-butter and simple small cakes. The christening cake may be as plain or as rich as you like, but it should be covered with all-white icing, appropriately decorated. The baby's mother cuts the cake, and everybody present should taste it.

The guests should leave as soon as tea is over . . . and their farewells should include some tactful and congratulatory speech about the baby !

There is no fee for a baptism, but parents who can afford to do so generally make an offering to one of the church funds. It is also usual to give the verger a tip.

Godparents who are well-to-do often give the baby's nurse a small present : a silver tip, perhaps, or a pair of gloves or handkerchiefs, might be presented by the godmother.

CHAPTER XV

MOURNING

EVERYTHING in any way connected with mourning should be done in the simplest manner possible.

When a death occurs in the family of a friend or near acquaintance, write a simple and quite brief note of sympathy, and send it as quickly as possible after you hear the news. Or you may simply leave your card at the house—do not go in—first writing on it " with deepest sympathy," or similar words. In the case of anyone whom you know only slightly, it is sufficient to leave your card.

The practice of sending round printed cards of thanks for the sympathy shown in a bereavement is steadily increasing, but it is still more correct, and infinitely more gracious, to answer personally all letters of condolence. Such notes may be very brief, there being no need for anything but an expression of appreciation of the sympathy received. They should be written as soon as possible after the funeral, and are usually on notepaper with a thin black edge. Heavily edged mourning stationery has quite gone out of use, and many people dispense with black edges altogether. To-day it is really a question of personal taste, rather than of correctness.

If you wish to send flowers, don't feel obliged to choose the formal white wreath which was once the only correct thing. You may select any flowers you prefer, and they can be made up in an informal sheaf quite as suitably as in any conventional design. They should reach the house not earlier than the day before the funeral. Leave with the florist a card which he will fasten to the flowers before sending them off. On this card you may write " With deep sympathy," " In affectionate remembrance," or any simple phrase which seems most suitable.

Naturally, when you know that the family particularly wish no flowers to be sent, you will observe this desire scrupulously.

When the first part of a funeral service takes place in a church, and the actual interment at a cemetery, it is usual for ordinary friends and acquaintances to attend at the church only, and not to follow on to the cemetery afterwards.

Don't pay a call of condolence before the funeral. Later you will receive a card or note of thanks for your sympathy, and after that it is correct to pay a short call. You need not wear black, although naturally you wouldn't choose a gay-coloured frock to go in. And don't, on any account, assume a sombre attitude. Be as natural as possible, and do not refer to the bereavement unless your hostess mentions it first.

Mourning clothes should be very simply cut, quite plain, and made from materials with a dull surface. Crêpe, heavy veils, black-bordered handkerchiefs, and other conspicuous signs of mourning are no longer customary. It is incorrect to wear jewellery with mourning.

The length of time that mourning should be worn becomes more and more a matter for one's own discretion. At one period mourning for wife, husband or child was worn for at least a year, but nowadays that period is often shortened considerably. A girl is not expected to wear mourning for her fiancé.

CHAPTER XVI

LETTER WRITING

To be legible is the first essential of any letter. This doesn't mean only that the handwriting should be clear and readable in itself, but that it should be on good paper . . . white or cream for preference . . . with a clear margin on either side, and the lines well and evenly spaced. It is just as grave a breach of good manners to send out a slovenly letter, carelessly written on a slightly soiled or crumpled sheet of paper, as it would be to speak or behave discourteously.

Garishly tinted paper, fancy or coloured edges, intricate and conspicuous monograms, or addresses printed in florid lettering must be left strictly alone, and stationery should on no account ever be scented.

Always date your letters. Be as punctilious about this for unimportant notes as for particular letters, so that it becomes an unbreakable habit. Put the date immediately under the address :

it is understood, isn't it, that " date " includes the day, month and year ?

When you write to a friend or an acquaintance, " Dear Mrs. So-and-So " is the correct beginning : to a particular friend or to a relation, " My dear . . . " is more generally used. Such letters should end " Yours sincerely," or " Yours very sincerely," according to the degree of friendship. This ending is used for all social correspondence, such as letters of invitation (which are dealt with in Chapter Five) and for friendly letters, but never for business or formal letters.

Business letters should begin " Dear Sir," or " Dear Madam," as the case may be : a business firm is often addressed simply " Gentlemen." Occasionally these letters begin " Sir " or " Madam," but the less stilted form is more commonly adopted nowadays. In answering a letter of this kind, however, take your cue from it, and if you are addressed " Madam," start your reply " Madam," likewise (or " Sir " as occasion demands).

All business letters may be closed with the phrase " Yours faithfully," which is the most correct one. (This should never be used for social letters.)

In signing a business letter to a stranger, do put your Christian name, not just an initial, before your surname, even if it is not your usual signature. It can be very embarrassing not to know whether your correspondent be a man or a woman, and handwriting isn't an infallible guide. In the same circumstances it is not only permissible, but often desirable, to put "(Mrs.)" or "(Miss)" . . . NEVER without brackets . . . before your name.

Keep your business letters concise and very much to the point, and be exceedingly careful about any dates mentioned in them. If, for example, you are making or confirming an appointment for an interview, mention the time, date and place, as you would in making a social engagement, and *do write very distinctly*. In confirming an appointment, repeat exactly the particulars given to you. It opens the way for all kinds of trouble and misunderstanding if you merely specify " next Wednesday " or " Monday week," without adding the day of the month and the month as well.

The third person is very seldom used nowadays in social correspondence, and then only between strangers. It is quite incorrect to use it when writing to anyone whom you have met, however slight the acquaintance. But it might be more convenient, for instance, in taking up a servant's reference than writing in the first person, though it is not essential. In such a communication the pronouns " you " and " I " must never be written, and no signature is added. Put the date in the lower left-hand corner.

Should you receive a third-person letter, answer it in the same manner. Should the strictly formal beginning, " Mrs. Blank presents her compliments," be used, start your answer with the same phrase.

The third person is also useful when ordering things from shops, engaging rooms, and so on, but in these cases any such social formality as " presenting compliments " is left out, and the request should be as brief and concise as possible. For example :

" Miss Henry would be obliged if Messrs. Stockall would send her by return . . . (whatever is needed). Miss Henry encloses postal order for (state the amount.)"

Don't slip into the bad mistake, half-way through, of writing " *I* enclose . . . "

When addressing an envelope to a married woman, remember to put *her husband's* Christian name or initial before the surname, and not her own. Write " Mrs. John Chant " or " Mrs. J. L. Chant," using the form by which the husband is best known. Addressing an unmarried woman, do not use her Christian name, except when she is a younger daughter, in which case the Christian name is always used to distinguish her from her elder sister.

In social correspondence a man is addressed, on an envelope, as Esquire . . . written " Esq,"

Be discreet when dealing with post cards, which should never bear anything at all private or personal. No beginning or ending phrases should be used on post cards. Start straight away with your message, as " We arrived here in good time," and at the end simply put your name. Many people make a practice of putting their initials only on a card.

CHAPTER XVII

THE FORMAL USE OF TITLES

(1) In Writing

THERE are certain definite rules for the formal use of titles when addressing communications to Royalty, nobility, and those of other ranks. For the purpose of reference the more important of these are given here.

A letter to the King or Queen would be addressed :

> *His Majesty*   or   *Her Majesty*
>   *The King*   *The Queen*

In point of fact, however, neither the King nor the Queen are written to directly, except by their personal friends. When it is desired to interest either of Their Majesties in a charity, for example, or to ask the favour of their presence on some special occasion, the correct procedure is to write to their respective secretaries, requesting that the matter shall be brought before them.

A communication to a member of the Royal Family should have written at the top of it " *To His Royal Highness the Duke (or Duchess) of*——" and begin " Sir." The ending would be :

> " *I have the honour to be*
>   *Your Royal Highness's most obedient*
>   *servant.*"

Address the envelope : " *H.R.H. The Duke of*——"

Other Royal Princes and Princesses are addressed in the same manner.

In writing to any royal personage never use the direct " you," but " *Your Royal Highness*," as : " *Should Your Royal Highness honour us by . . .*" etc.

To a Duke, a formal letter would begin " *My Lord Duke* " and end " *Your Grace's most obedient servant*," the envelope being addressed :

> *His Grace*
> *The Duke of Blankshire.*

To a Duchess, begin " *Madam*," using the same concluding phrase as to a Duke. Her title should be written above the " Madam," and the envelope bear the address :

> *Her Grace*
> *The Duchess of Blankshire.*

To a Marquis or Marchioness, begin " *My Lord Marquis* " or " *My Lady*," and end, in the first instance, " *I have the honour to be, My Lord Marquis, your most obedient servant,*" and in the second : " *I have the honour to be, Your Ladyship's most obedient servant.*"   Address the envelope " *The Most Hon. the Marquis (or Marchioness) of . . .* "

Make quite sure, first, of the correct title of the Marquis addressed : you will find it in any " Peerage."   It may be the Marquis *of* So-and-So, or The Marquis So-and-So, and it is a serious, but quite common, mistake to insert " of " when it should not be there.

To an Earl or Countess, begin " *My Lord* " or " *Madam*," and conclude " *I have the honour to be, My Lord (or Madam) your faithful servant.*"   Address the envelope : " *The Right Hon. the Earl (or Countess) of . . .* "   The same rule applies to these titles as to that of Marquis : make sure about the " of " first of all.

Use the same opening, and address the envelope in the same fashion, to a Viscount, Viscountess, Baron or Baroness.   In the case of Baron or Baroness, the envelope should be addressed : *The Right Hon. The Lord . . .* or *The Right Hon. The Lady . . .*

On envelopes addressed to noblemen or their wives the title should be written thus :

| *The Most Hon.* | *The Right Hon.* |
| *The Marquis* . . . | *The Viscountess* . . |

and not in a single line.

In addressing the daughters or younger sons of Dukes, Marquises or Earls, the Christian name must never be omitted after their courtesy titles. The daughters of Dukes, Marquises and Earls have the title " *Lady* " prefixed to their Christian name and family surname, as " *Lady Mary Aldwych*," and it would be quite incorrect to write (or say) " *Lady Aldwych* " without the Christian name. The wife of a Knight may be " *Lady So-and-So*," but when the Christian name is added, it indicates that the possessor of the title is the daughter of Duke, Marquis or Earl, and marks an important distinction.

The younger sons of Dukes and Marquises take the title of " *Lord*," which is prefixed to Christian name and family surname. Here, again, the Christian name must always be used.

The younger sons of Earls, and the sons and daughters of Viscounts and Barons all have the courtesy title "*Honourable*" before their Christian name and family surname. This title, however, is used only on envelopes addressed to them, and never on visiting cards, or when they are spoken to. One would write "*The Hon. George Brown*" or "*The Hon. Alicia Jones*," but in speaking one should say "*Mr. Brown*" or "*Miss Jones.*" The "Mr." or "Miss" are never used after "The Hon." in writing, remember. The wife of an "Honourable" should be addressed as *The Hon. Mrs.*

Do not write the word "Honourable" in full, but as "*Hon.*", and always put "The" before it.

To a Baronet or Knight or their wives, begin your letter "*Sir*" or "*Madam.*" On the envelope write: "*Sir Charles . . . Bt.*", or "*Lady . . .*" when addressing a Baronet or his wife. A Knight is addressed as "*Sir Peter . . . K.C.B.*," (or whatever letters he is entitled to) and his wife as "*Lady . . .*" A Knight Bachelor has no letters after his name.

You may have noticed that sometimes the widow of a Peer or Baronet uses her Christian name before her title, as "*Evelyn, Countess of . . .*" This is to distinguish her from the wife of the present holder of the title, and is chosen by her in place of the title of " *The Dowager Countess of . . .* "

Privy Councillors have the title " *The Right Hon.*" prefixed to their names on their letters, and " *P.C.*" after them.

Communications to Members of Parliament should have the letters " M.P." after the name : " *T. Hunt, Esq., M.P.*"

When writing to an Archbishop, begin " *Your Grace,*" and address the envelope " *His Grace the Archbishop of . . .* " A formal letter to a Bishop begins " *My Lord* " (friends would write to him as " Dear Bishop "), the envelope being addressed : " *The Right Rev. the Lord Bishop of . . .* "

To a Dean a formal or friendly letter may begin " *Dear Mr. Dean,*" and would be addressed : " *The Very Rev. the Dean of . . .* " To Rector, Vicar or Curate the more formal letters begin : " *Reverend Sir ;* " others, " *Dear Mr. . . .* " On the envelope write : " *The Rev. James . . . ,*" never omitting the Christian name or initials. All ministers of religion, by courtesy, are addressed as " Rev."

A Lord Mayor or Lady Mayoress is addressed on envelopes as " *The Right Hon. the Lord Mayor of . . .* " or " *The Right Hon. the Lady*

Mayoress." Begin the letter " My Lord " or
" Madam." A Mayor is addressed as " The
Mayor of . . . " (or on formal communications
as " His Worship the Mayor of . . . "), and a
letter to him begins " Sir."

All officers in Navy or Army (with the exception of Army Lieutenants, who are addressed
as Esq., with the letters indicating their
regiment) should have their rank prefixed to
their names on envelopes addressed to them.
The rank and name of any Naval officer should
be followed by the letters " R.N."

When writing to a medical man, remember
that a surgeon is addressed on the envelope as
" J. Green, Esq.," the letters to which he is
entitled following the name, and a physician
as " Dr. Green." Begin your letter to the
surgeon " Dear Sir," or " Dear Mr. Green,"
and to the physician, " Dear Sir " or " Dear
Dr. Green." End the letters beginning " Dear
Sir," with " Yours faithfully ; " the others,
" Yours sincerely."

(2) Personal Forms of Address

Should you have the privilege of being introduced to Royalty, there is no need at all for you
to feel anxious about the correct thing to do

or say, since the royal personage takes the initiative throughout.

When the introduction is made you should simply bow (or curtsey). Never make any movement to shake hands unless the royal personage offers first to do so, and do not speak until you are spoken to, then answer as simply and naturally as possible.

His Majesty the King is addressed as " Your Majesty," and Her Majesty the Queen in the same manner : the Prince of Wales and all Royal Princes as " Sir " : Royal Princesses and the wives of Royal Princes as " Ma'am."

Should a question be asked in the course of conversation with a Royal Prince or Princess, however, the direct " you " must always be avoided, and the phrase " Your Royal Highness " used instead, as : " Has Your Royal Highness seen . . . ? " The same applies to any reference made to the royal personage in his or her presence, as : " Her Royal Highness is particularly interested in . . . "

A Duke or Duchess is addressed as " Duke " or " Duchess " by those whom they meet socially, and as " Your Grace " by others.

The members of the British peerage generally are addressed as " Lord . . . " or " Lady . . . "

H

by their friends and acquaintances : as " My Lord " or " My Lady " by any not on a social equality.

Those who bear the courtesy title of " Honourable " are spoken to as " Mr. . . . ," " Mrs. . . . " or " Miss . . . " as the case may be. The title is not used even in announcing them when they enter a room.

In addressing Baronets and Knights the title " Sir " is prefixed to their Christian name, and the surname is not used, as, " Sir Charles." Their wives are known as " Lady So-and-So," using the surname only. Their Christian name must *not* be used, this being given only in the case of daughters of a Duke, Marquis or Earl. By servants and tradespeople they are addressed as " My Lady."

An Archbishop is addressed as " Your Grace," and a Bishop as " My Lord " : a Dean is given his clerical title and surname, and so is an Archdeacon. Clergymen are addressed as " Mr. . . . ," or " Father " when this is more usual, without the surname.

Address Naval or Army officers by rank and surname, remembering that a Lieutenant-Colonel is addressed as " Colonel So-and-So," and a Lieutenant in the Army as " Mr. So-and-So."

Correct Pronunciation of Surnames

There is such a difference between the spelling and the pronunciation of many surnames that you may well be puzzled at times as to how this or that name is pronounced. The following list will be useful on these occasions.

SPELLING	PRONUNCIATION
Abergavenny	Abergenny
Arundel	Arrandel
Baring	Bearing
Beaconsfield	Beckonsfield
Beauchamp	Beecham
Belvoir	Beaver
Berkeley	Barkley
Bertie	Bartie
Bethune	Beeton
Bicester	Bister
Blount	Blunt
Blyth or Blythe	Bly or Blyth
Bourchier	Bowcher
Bourke	Burk
Brougham	Broum
Buchan	Buck-an or Buch-an
Charteris	Charters

SPELLING	PRONUNCIATION
Chisholm	Chizum
Cholmondeley	Chumley
Cockburn	Coburn
Coghlan	Colan
Colquhoun	Kohoon
Coutts	Koots
Cowper	Cooper
Dalziel	Dee-ell
Derby	Darby
Des Vaux	Deveu
Devereux	Devereu
Donoghue	Dunnohew
Duchesne	Dukarn
Elgin	Elgin (g as in " goat ")
Eyre	Air
Falconer	Fawkner
Farquhar	Farkar
Ffolliott	Folliott
Fortescue	Fortiskew
Geoffrey	Jefrey
Gifford	Jifford or Gifford
Gillett	Gillett (g as in " gate ")

SPELLING	PRONUNCIATION
Glamis	Glams
Gough	Goff
Gower	Gore
Harcourt	Harkut
Hawarden	Harden
Heathcote	Heth-kut
Hepburn	Hebburn
Hertford	Harford
Home	Hume
Inglis	Ingells
Jervis	Jarvis
Kirkcudbright	Kirkoobry
Knollys	Nowles
Leconfield	Lekonfield
Lefevre	Le-fever
Leigh	Lee
Leveson-Gower	Looson-Gore
Lyvedon	Liveden
McIntosh	Makintosh
McLeod	McCloud
Mainwaring	Mannering
Marjoribanks	Marshbanks
Meiklejohn	Micklejohn
Menzies	Myng-ies

SPELLING	PRONUNCIATION
Meux	Mews
Milngavie	Mulguy
Monckton	Munkton
Montgomery	Mungumery
Mowbray	Mobrey
Nigel	Ni-jel
Pepys	Peeps
Ponsonby	Punsonby
Pontefract	Pomfret or Pontefract
Pugh	Pew
Pytchley	Py-tchley
Ruthven	Riven
St. Clair	Sinclair
St. John	Sinjin
St. Leger	Selinger
St. Maur	See-mor or S'nt Maur
Sandys	Sands
Scrimgeour	Skrim-jer
Seymour	Seymer
Strachan	Strawn or Strach-an
Thynne	Thin
Tollemache	Tollmash

SPELLING	PRONUNCIATION
Tyrrwhitt	Tirritt
Urquhart	Erk-art
Vaughan	Von
Villiers	Villers
Waldegrave	Walgrave
Wemyss	Weems
Willoughby D'Eresby	Willowby D'Ersby

LITTLE COURTESIES THAT COUNT

If you meet a friend in the street and wish to speak to her, it is more courteous to turn and walk along with her as you talk, than to keep her standing where you meet. It also causes much less inconvenience to passers-by.

When walking with a man, remember that your place is on the inside of the pavement. Naturally, it is the man's duty to take the outside as a matter of course, but the woman who instinctively moves to the inside makes this much easier for him.

When you are with another woman and a man, always let the elder woman walk next to the man, who will take the outside position.

Should you be walking with a man who meets a man friend whom you do not know, the stranger will raise his hat as a matter of courtesy in recognising your escort, but it is incorrect for you to bow or make any acknowledgment.

A girl or young woman should always offer her seat to an elderly man or woman, anyone of any age who is crippled or obviously looks ill, or a woman with a small child in arms, when in a crowded train, tram or bus. But be very tactful in the case of an older woman : many a woman who has never thought of herself as approaching the elderly stage has received a disagreeable shock when offered a seat by a younger woman. She would *much* rather have been left strap-hanging all day !

When offered such a courtesy yourself, never take it as a matter of course, nor with a muttered " Thanks." A pleasant smile and " Thank you " are due, but there is no need to go beyond that.

The same rule applies if anyone—man, woman or child—picks up anything you have dropped, or left behind in train, restaurant or on any other occasion. Smile, and say " Thank you."

But the service does not warrant entering into conversation.

Never omit to thank a servant for any special little service rendered, and to say " Please " and " Thank you " as conscientiously as you would to anyone else.

INDEX